Mythical Creatures

Dianne Irving
Illustrated by Rob Kiely

Contents

What is a Mythical Creature?

Have you ever heard of a horse that can fly or a beast that breathes fire? There are many amazing **mythical** creatures, such as dragons, genies and griffins.

Some people might believe that mythical creatures are real, but they're not. What we know about mythical creatures comes from stories that have been told for a very long time. These stories come from all over the world.

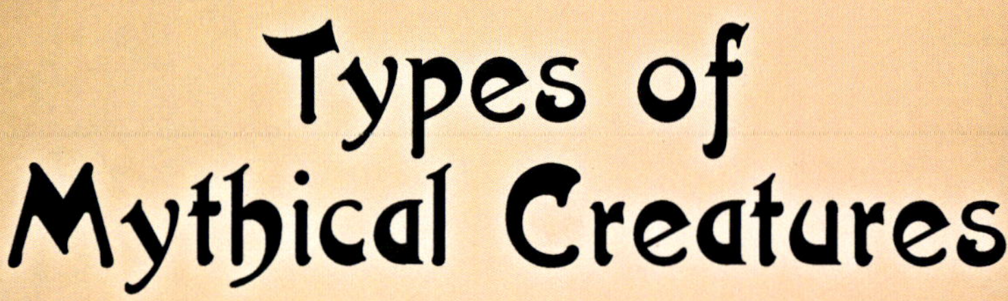

Types of Mythical Creatures

There are many different kinds of mythical creatures.

Some are like people, such as a giant or troll. Others are like animals, such as a unicorn or phoenix.

Some mythical creatures are part person and part animal. The mermaid has the head and body of a person and the tail of a fish.

Let's take a look at some more weird and wonderful mythical creatures.

Thunderbird

The thunderbird is a giant bird with huge wings. Stories about the thunderbird come from the indigenous peoples of North America.

The thunderbird is very clever and powerful. It lives at the top of high mountains.

Some stories say that when the thunderbird gets angry it causes storms. It makes thunder by beating its wings and lightning by blinking its eyes. Other stories say the thunderbird is good, and protects people.

Some stories say it carries a lake on its back and that is where rain comes from. These stories say that the thunderbird made it rain so the plants would grow.

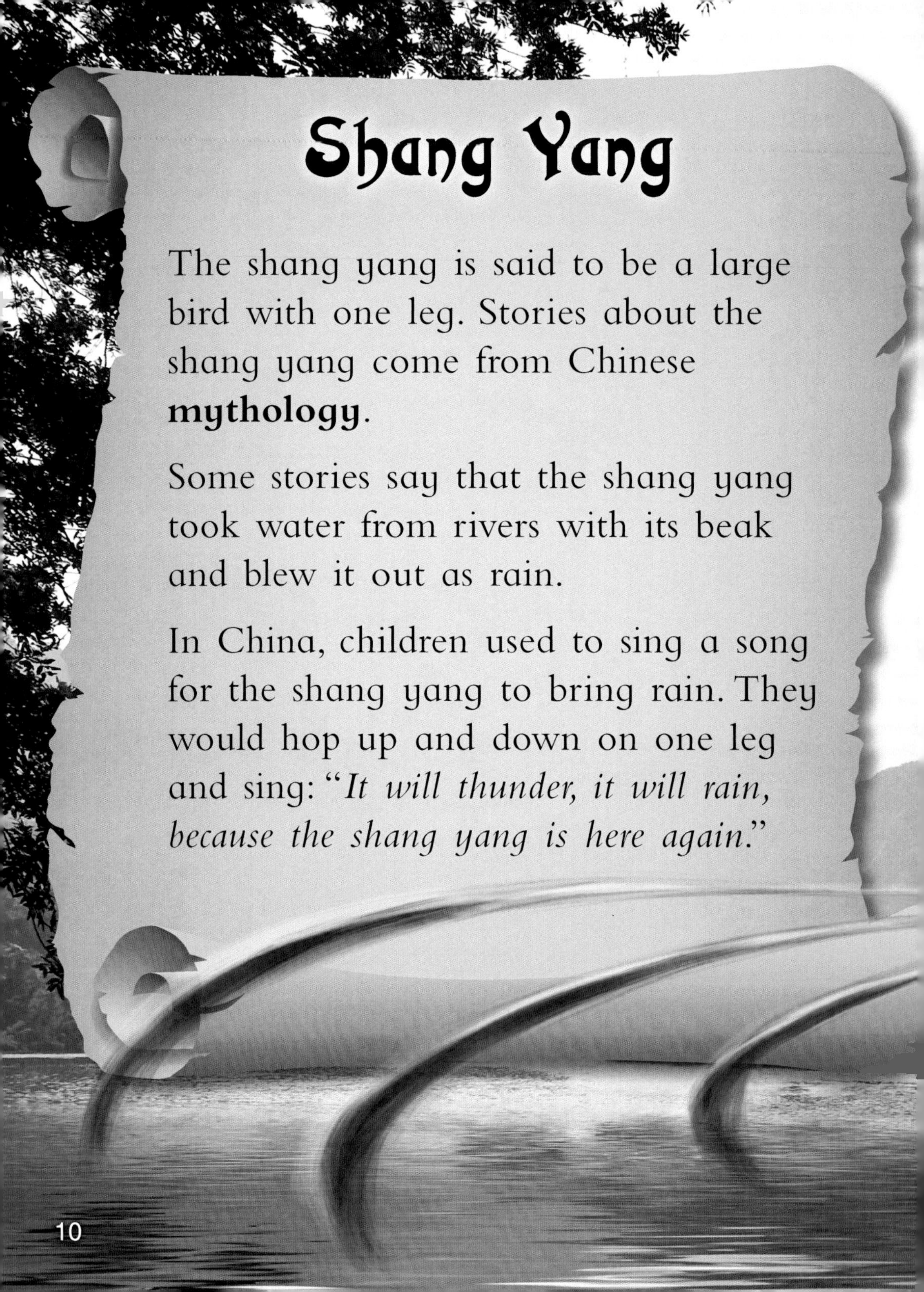

Shang Yang

The shang yang is said to be a large bird with one leg. Stories about the shang yang come from Chinese **mythology**.

Some stories say that the shang yang took water from rivers with its beak and blew it out as rain.

In China, children used to sing a song for the shang yang to bring rain. They would hop up and down on one leg and sing: "*It will thunder, it will rain, because the shang yang is here again.*"

In one story, the shang yang went to a palace to warn the people about a storm. The people built walls and dug drains to get ready for the storm.

The storm came. It rained and rained. All of the land around the palace flooded, but the palace did not flood. The shang yang had helped the people to save their palace.

Bunyip

If you hear a terrible roar near a **waterhole**, it just might be a bunyip. Bunyips come from the myths of Aboriginal people in Australia. Bunyips live in rivers, lakes, swamps and **billabongs**. Stories say that bunyips eat people and animals that come into their home.

There are many descriptions of what the bunyip might look like. Aboriginal people believed it could be covered in scales or fur. Early European settlers believed it could have a tail like a horse, tusks like a walrus or even fins!

Some people think that stories about the bunyip may have come from stories about a real animal called the diprotodon. The diprotodon was a giant **marsupial** that became **extinct** about 20 000 years ago.

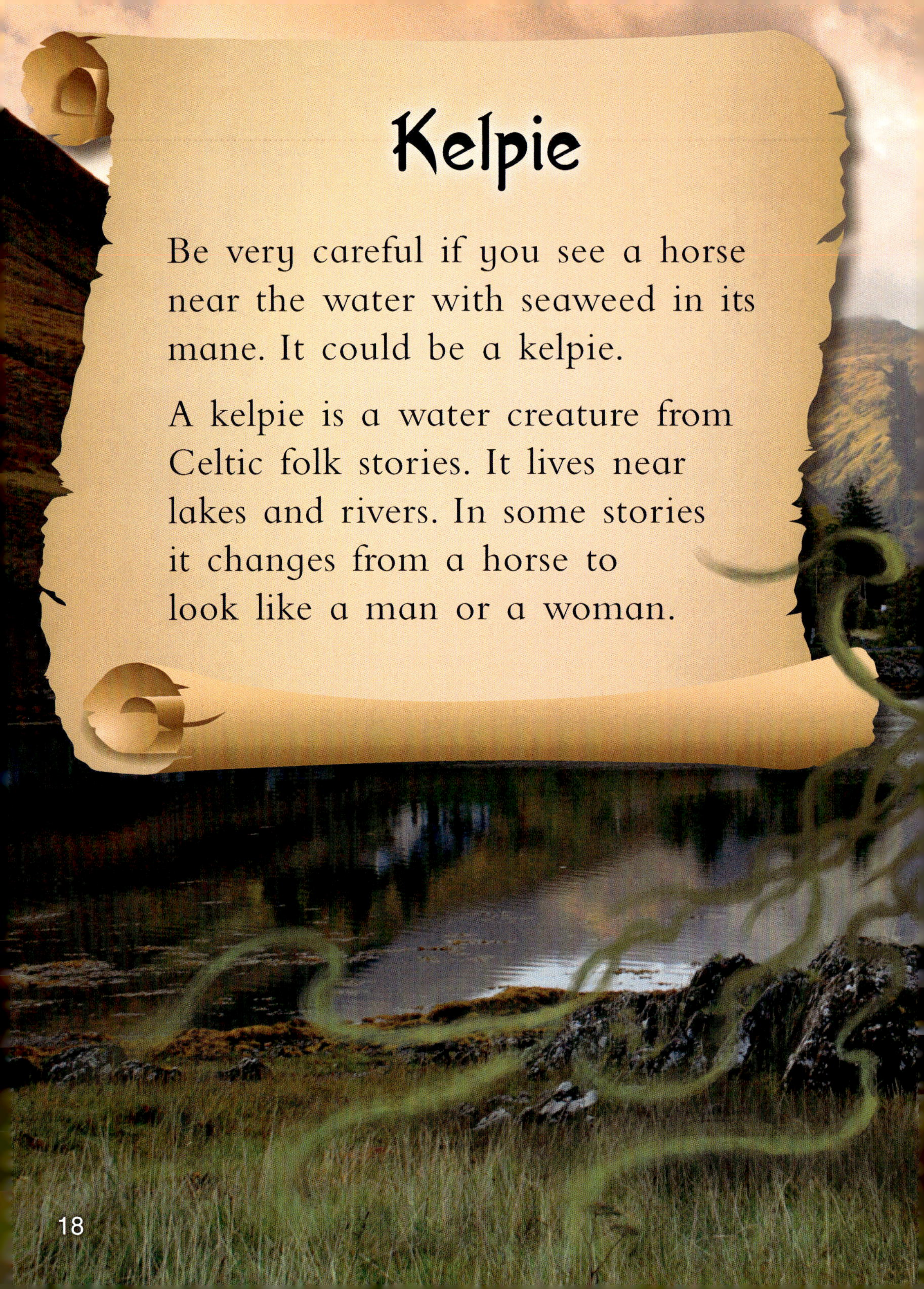

Kelpie

Be very careful if you see a horse near the water with seaweed in its mane. It could be a kelpie.

A kelpie is a water creature from Celtic folk stories. It lives near lakes and rivers. In some stories it changes from a horse to look like a man or a woman.

Stories tell how kelpies pretended to be lost to trick people into getting on their backs. Once the person was on their back, the kelpie would run into the water. It would slap the water with its tail, making a sound like thunder! The horse and rider would disappear, never to be seen again.

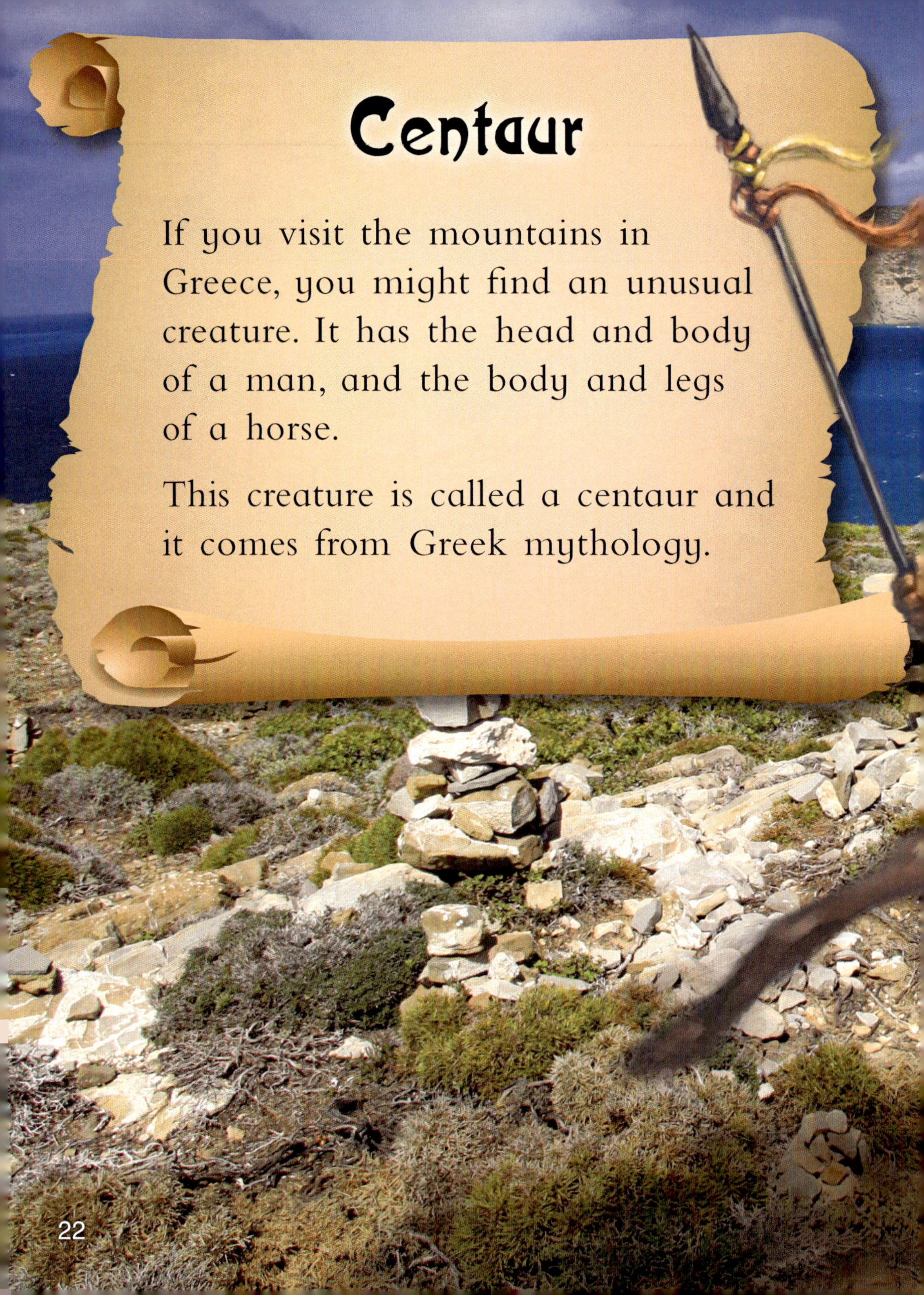

Centaur

If you visit the mountains in Greece, you might find an unusual creature. It has the head and body of a man, and the body and legs of a horse.

This creature is called a centaur and it comes from Greek mythology.

Most stories tell of centaurs as being very unfriendly, but there was one centaur who was different to the rest. His name was Chiron and he was very kind and clever.

Chiron knew a lot about medicine, music and hunting. He was also a great teacher.

Nuwa

Nuwa is a goddess from Chinese mythology. It is thought that Nuwa came to the world before there were any other people.

Some people think that Nuwa was a beautiful woman. Other people think that she had the head of a woman and the body of a snake.

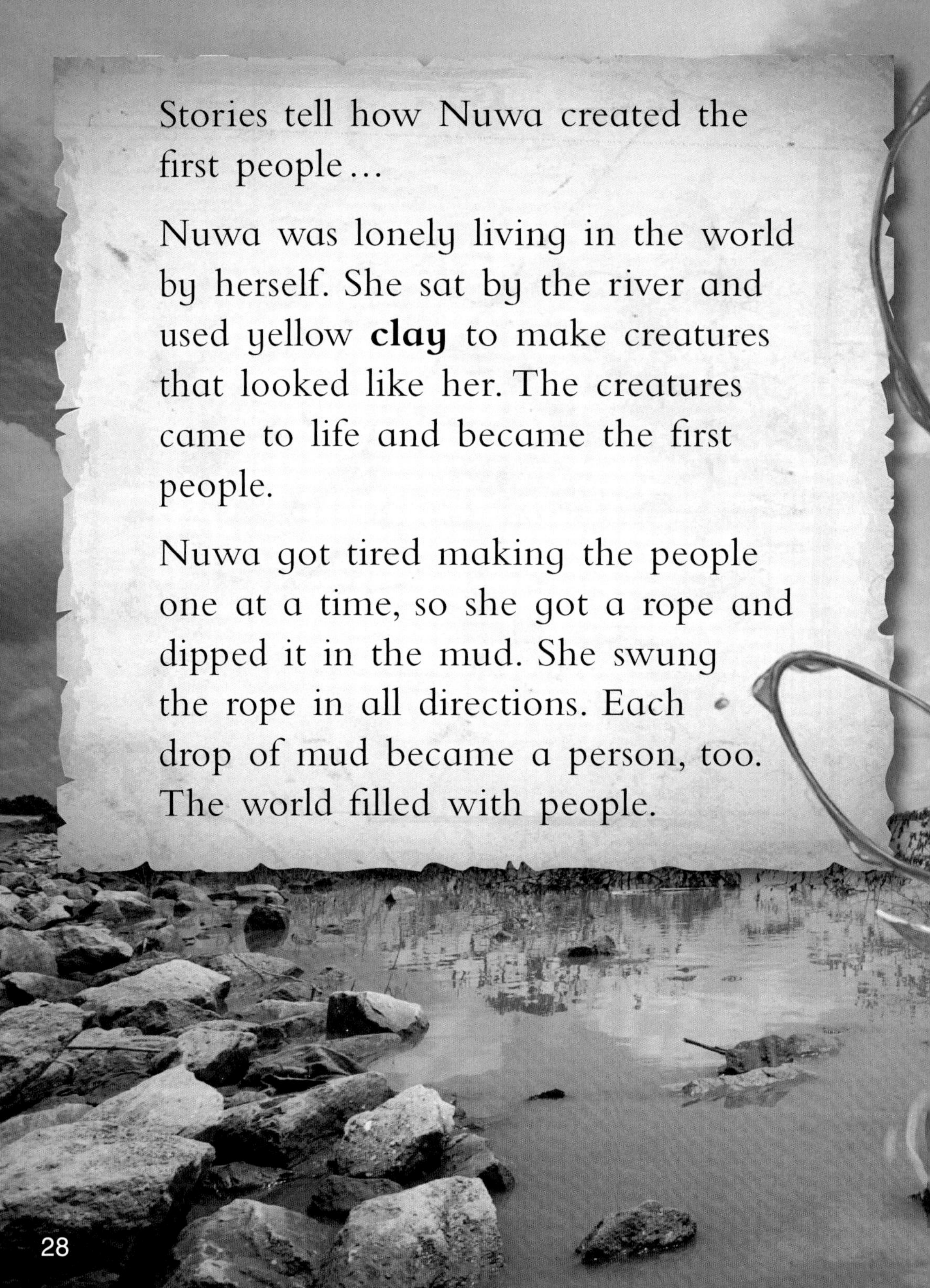

Stories tell how Nuwa created the first people…

Nuwa was lonely living in the world by herself. She sat by the river and used yellow **clay** to make creatures that looked like her. The creatures came to life and became the first people.

Nuwa got tired making the people one at a time, so she got a rope and dipped it in the mud. She swung the rope in all directions. Each drop of mud became a person, too. The world filled with people.

Quiz

1 Are mythical creatures real?

2 What is a mythical creature that can change to look like a person?

3 What country does the story of Nuwa come from?

4 Are centaurs usually friendly?

5 How does a thunderbird make lightning?

6 Which mythical creature lives in a waterhole?

7 Which mythical creature only has one leg?

Answers: **1** No **2** Kelpie **3** China **4** No **5** By blinking **6** Bunyip **7** Shang Yang

Glossary

billabongs pools of water (or waterholes) that only form during floods

clay earth or mud that sets hard when dry

extinct no longer existing

marsupial a type of mammal that drinks milk from a female when young

mythical exists only in myths or stories; not real

mythology a collection of myths belonging to a group of people

waterhole a small pool of water that has formed naturally